ZERO WASTE

Monthly and Weekly planner

THIS NOTEBOOK BELONGS TO:

.

_____

YEAR_____

Waste isn't waste
Until
We waste it

ZERO WASTE

According to some estimates, if we continue on our current path, the oceans will contain more plastic than fish by the year 2050.
We've produced as much plastic in the past decade as we did in the entire twentieth century. We're drowning in the stuff, and we need to start making some hard choices.
There are thousands of books that explain why not to use plastic or to have a zero-waste life, but the truth is that none of those books actually get you into action.
This planner is made for you to start changing the world from today.

In this book, you will find:

1. 30 Tips on how to live life without plastic.

2. Guided templates to fill with your zero waste plan for:

Beauty
Kitchen
Bathroom
Cleaning
Sweet time
Eco gifts
Clothes
Emails
Christmas time
Books and blogs
Party decorations
Shops
Travel
Plastic counter

3. Monthly planner

4. Weekly planner – undated so it can be used at any time in the future.

Every small step matters when it is related to reducing plastic waste. Start today!

BEAUTY
Homemade Beauty Tricks

PRODUCTS

List of products that I can buy in bulk

_____

_____

_____

_____

_____

_____

_____

_____

_____

_____

_____

_____

_____

_____

_____

_____

_____

_____

_____

_____

_____

KITCHEN

Ideas for a Zero waste kitchen

_____

_____

_____

_____

_____

_____

_____

_____

_____

_____

_____

_____

_____

_____

_____

_____

_____

_____

_____

_____

_____

BATHROOM

Ideas for a Zero waste fathroom

_____

_____

_____

_____

_____

_____

_____

_____

_____

_____

_____

_____

_____

_____

_____

_____

_____

_____

_____

_____

CLEANING

 *Homemade cleaning products recipes*

SWEET TIME!

Ideas for Zero waste desserts

_____
_____
_____
_____
_____
_____
_____
_____
_____
_____
_____
_____
_____
_____
_____
_____
_____
_____
_____
_____
_____
_____

ECO GIFTS

Eco-friendly gifts for special occasions

NOTES

CLOTHES

List of new clothes I buy

Questions to ask myself

Do I really need this? Can I buy it second-hand? Has this been ethically manufactured?

Date   What

_____   _____

_____   _____

_____   _____

_____   _____

_____   _____

_____   _____

_____   _____

_____   _____

_____   _____

_____   _____

_____   _____

_____   _____

_____   _____

EMAILS

Sent to ask companies to save the world:

I.e.: to change packaging
Ask for transparency of ingredients...

Date	To

CHRISTMAS TIME!

Tree decoration ideas

_____

_____

_____

_____

_____

_____

_____

_____

_____

_____

_____

_____

_____

_____

_____

_____

_____

_____

PARTY DECORATIONS

Ideas of recycled ornaments

_____
_____
_____
_____
_____
_____
_____
_____
_____
_____
_____

_____
_____
_____
_____
_____
_____
_____
_____
_____
_____
_____

LEARN MORE
About living a Zero waste life

Books to read

_____

_____

_____

_____

_____

_____

_____

_____

_____

_____

_____

_____

_____

_____

Blogs to follow

_____

_____

_____

_____

_____

_____

_____

_____

_____

_____

_____

_____

_____

_____

SHOPS

Sustainable shops

Bulk food

_____
_____
_____
_____
_____
_____
_____
_____
_____
_____
_____
_____
_____
_____
_____
_____
_____
_____

TRAVEL

tips on traveling not harming the earth

_____   _____

_____   _____

_____   _____

_____   _____

_____   _____

_____   _____

_____   _____

_____   _____

_____   _____

_____   _____

_____   _____

_____   _____

_____   _____

_____   _____

_____   _____

_____   _____

PLASTIC COUNTER

Pick a random day and count how many times you use single-use plastic

_____   _____
_____   _____
_____   _____
_____   _____
_____   _____
_____   _____
_____   _____
_____   _____
_____   _____
_____   _____
_____   _____
_____   _____
_____   _____
_____   _____
_____   _____
_____   _____

TIPS ON HOW TO LIVE A ZERO WASTE LIFE:

- SAY NO TO FROZEN FOOD AND SINGLE-SERVING SIZES

- ASK COMPANIES TO CHANGE THEIR PACKAGING

- CHOOSE REUSABLE CLOTH SANDWICH/SNACK BAGS

- CHOOSE STAINLESS STEEL ICE CUBE TRAYS AND POPSICLE MOLDS

- AVOID DISPOSABLE PLASTIC PENS

- CHOOSE PET TOYS AND FURNITURE MADE FROM NATURAL MATERIALS

- AVOID BUYING NEW PLASTIC CLOTHING (POLYESTER, ACRYLIC, LYCRA)

- THROW A ZERO-WASTE PARTY

- CONSIDER GIVING CHARITABLE GIFT CARDS

- GROCERY SHOPPING WITH LESS PLASTIC

- FIND WAYS TO WRAP GIFTS WITHOUT PLASTIC TAPE

- REQUEST ZERO PLASTIC PACKAGING WHEN ORDERING ONLINE

- SUPPORT SMALL AND LOCAL BUSINESSES

- BUY SECOND-HAND

- EXPLORE PLASTIC-FREE HAIR ACCESSORIES

- **USE PLASTIC-FREE FOOD CONTAINERS**

- **BRING YOUR OWN CUP**

- **SAY NO TO PLASTIC STRAWS**

- **BE A MINIMALIST**

- **USE A WATER FILTER SYSTEM**

- **START YOUR OWN PLASTIC-FREE CAMPAIGN**

- **CARRY REUSABLE SHOPPING BAGS**

- **CARRY A STAINLESS-STEEL TRAVEL MUG**

- **TREAT YOURSELF TO AN ICE CREAM CONE**

- **SHOP AT YOUR LOCAL FARMERS MARKET**

- **BUY FRESH BREAD THAT COMES IN EITHER PAPER BAGS OR NO BAGS**

- **BUY LARGE WHEELS OF UNWRAPPED CHEESE**

- **CLEAN WITH VINEGAR AND WATER**

- **USE POWDERED DISHWASHER DETERGENT IN A CARDBOARD BOX**

- **SWITCH TO BAR SOAP INSTEAD OF LIQUID SOAP**

MONTHLY PLANNER

MONTH:_____

SUN	MON	TUE	WED	THU	FRI	SAT

NOTES

MONTH:_____

SUN	MON	TUE	WED	THU	FRI	SAT

NOTES

MONTH:_____

SUN	MON	TUE	WED	THU	FRI	SAT

NOTES

MONTH:_____

SUN	MON	TUE	WED	THU	FRI	SAT

NOTES

MONTH:_____

SUN	MON	TUE	WED	THU	FRI	SAT

NOTES

_____   _____

_____   _____

_____   _____

_____   _____

_____   _____

_____   _____

_____   _____

_____   _____

_____   _____

_____   _____

_____   _____

_____   _____

_____   _____

_____   _____

_____   _____

_____   _____

MONTH:_____

SUN	MON	TUE	WED	THU	FRI	SAT

NOTES

_____   _____

_____   _____

_____   _____

_____   _____

_____   _____

_____   _____

_____   _____

_____   _____

_____   _____

_____   _____

_____   _____

_____   _____

_____   _____

_____   _____

_____   _____

_____   _____

_____   _____

MONTH:_____

SUN	MON	TUE	WED	THU	FRI	SAT

NOTES

MONTH:_____

SUN	MON	TUE	WED	THU	FRI	SAT

NOTES

MONTH:_____

SUN	MON	TUE	WED	THU	FRI	SAT

NOTES

MONTH:_____

SUN	MON	TUE	WED	THU	FRI	SAT

NOTES

_____   _____

_____   _____

_____   _____

_____   _____

_____   _____

_____   _____

_____   _____

_____   _____

_____   _____

_____   _____

_____   _____

_____   _____

_____   _____

_____   _____

_____   _____

_____   _____

_____   _____

_____   _____

MONTH:_____

SUN	MON	TUE	WED	THU	FRI	SAT

NOTES

_____   _____

_____   _____

_____   _____

_____   _____

_____   _____

_____   _____

_____   _____

_____   _____

_____   _____

_____   _____

_____   _____

_____   _____

_____   _____

_____   _____

_____   _____

_____   _____

_____   _____

MONTH:_____

SUN	MON	TUE	WED	THU	FRI	SAT

NOTES

WEEKLY PLANNER

○ MONDAY

SUSTAINABLE ACTIONS

○ TUESDAY

○ WEDNESDAY

TO DO

○ THURSDAY

○ FRIDAY

○ SATURDAY / SUNDAY

○ MONDAY

SUSTAINABLE ACTIONS

○ TUESDAY

○ WEDNESDAY

TO DO

○ THURSDAY

○ FRIDAY

○ SATURDAY / SUNDAY

○ MONDAY

SUSTAINABLE ACTIONS

○ TUESDAY

○ WEDNESDAY

TO DO

○ THURSDAY

○ FRIDAY

○ SATURDAY / SUNDAY

○ MONDAY

SUSTAINABLE ACTIONS

○ TUESDAY

○ WEDNESDAY

TO DO

○ THURSDAY

○ FRIDAY

○ SATURDAY / SUNDAY

○ MONDAY

○ TUESDAY

○ WEDNESDAY

○ THURSDAY

○ FRIDAY

○ SATURDAY / SUNDAY

SUSTAINABLE ACTIONS

TO DO

○ MONDAY

SUSTAINABLE ACTIONS

○ TUESDAY

○ WEDNESDAY

TO DO

○ THURSDAY

○ FRIDAY

○ SATURDAY / SUNDAY

○ MONDAY

SUSTAINABLE ACTIONS

○ TUESDAY

○ WEDNESDAY

TO DO

○ THURSDAY

○ FRIDAY

○ SATURDAY / SUNDAY

○ MONDAY

SUSTAINABLE ACTIONS

○ TUESDAY

○ WEDNESDAY

TO DO

○ THURSDAY

○ FRIDAY

○ SATURDAY / SUNDAY

○ MONDAY

SUSTAINABLE ACTIONS

○ TUESDAY

○ WEDNESDAY

TO DO

○ THURSDAY

○ FRIDAY

○ SATURDAY / SUNDAY

○ MONDAY

SUSTAINABLE ACTIONS

○ TUESDAY

○ WEDNESDAY

TO DO

○ THURSDAY

○ FRIDAY

○ SATURDAY / SUNDAY

○ MONDAY

SUSTAINABLE ACTIONS

○ TUESDAY

○ WEDNESDAY

TO DO

○ THURSDAY

○ FRIDAY

○ SATURDAY / SUNDAY

○ MONDAY

SUSTAINABLE ACTIONS

○ TUESDAY

○ WEDNESDAY

TO DO

○ THURSDAY

○ FRIDAY

○ SATURDAY / SUNDAY

○ MONDAY

○ TUESDAY

○ WEDNESDAY

○ THURSDAY

○ FRIDAY

○ SATURDAY / SUNDAY

SUSTAINABLE ACTIONS

TO DO

○ MONDAY

SUSTAINABLE ACTIONS

○ TUESDAY

○ WEDNESDAY

TO DO

○ THURSDAY

○ FRIDAY

○ SATURDAY / SUNDAY

○ MONDAY

SUSTAINABLE ACTIONS

○ TUESDAY

○ WEDNESDAY

TO DO

○ THURSDAY

○ FRIDAY

○ SATURDAY / SUNDAY

○ MONDAY

SUSTAINABLE ACTIONS

○ TUESDAY

○ WEDNESDAY

TO DO

○ THURSDAY

○ FRIDAY

○ SATURDAY / SUNDAY

○ MONDAY

SUSTAINABLE ACTIONS

_____

_____

○ TUESDAY

_____

_____

_____

_____

○ WEDNESDAY

TO DO

_____

○ THURSDAY

_____

_____

_____

_____

○ FRIDAY

_____

_____

_____

_____

○ SATURDAY / SUNDAY

_____

_____

_____

○ MONDAY

SUSTAINABLE ACTIONS

○ TUESDAY

○ WEDNESDAY

TO DO

○ THURSDAY

○ FRIDAY

○ SATURDAY / SUNDAY

○ MONDAY

SUSTAINABLE ACTIONS

○ TUESDAY

○ WEDNESDAY

TO DO

○ THURSDAY

○ FRIDAY

○ SATURDAY / SUNDAY

○ MONDAY

SUSTAINABLE ACTIONS

○ TUESDAY

○ WEDNESDAY

TO DO

○ THURSDAY

○ FRIDAY

○ SATURDAY / SUNDAY

○ MONDAY

SUSTAINABLE ACTIONS

○ TUESDAY

○ WEDNESDAY

TO DO

○ THURSDAY

○ FRIDAY

○ SATURDAY / SUNDAY

○ MONDAY

SUSTAINABLE ACTIONS

○ TUESDAY

○ WEDNESDAY

TO DO

○ THURSDAY

○ FRIDAY

○ SATURDAY / SUNDAY

○ MONDAY

SUSTAINABLE ACTIONS

○ TUESDAY

○ WEDNESDAY

TO DO

○ THURSDAY

○ FRIDAY

○ SATURDAY / SUNDAY

○ MONDAY

○ TUESDAY

○ WEDNESDAY

○ THURSDAY

○ FRIDAY

○ SATURDAY / SUNDAY

SUSTAINABLE ACTIONS

TO DO

○ MONDAY

○ TUESDAY

○ WEDNESDAY

○ THURSDAY

○ FRIDAY

○ SATURDAY / SUNDAY

SUSTAINABLE ACTIONS

TO DO

○ MONDAY

SUSTAINABLE ACTIONS

○ TUESDAY

○ WEDNESDAY

TO DO

○ THURSDAY

○ FRIDAY

○ SATURDAY / SUNDAY

○ MONDAY

○ TUESDAY

○ WEDNESDAY

○ THURSDAY

○ FRIDAY

○ SATURDAY / SUNDAY

SUSTAINABLE ACTIONS

TO DO

○ MONDAY

SUSTAINABLE ACTIONS

○ TUESDAY

○ WEDNESDAY

TO DO

○ THURSDAY

○ FRIDAY

○ SATURDAY / SUNDAY

○ MONDAY

SUSTAINABLE ACTIONS

○ TUESDAY

○ WEDNESDAY

TO DO

○ THURSDAY

○ FRIDAY

○ SATURDAY / SUNDAY

○ MONDAY

SUSTAINABLE ACTIONS

○ TUESDAY

○ WEDNESDAY

TO DO

○ THURSDAY

○ FRIDAY

○ SATURDAY / SUNDAY

○ MONDAY

SUSTAINABLE ACTIONS

○ TUESDAY

○ WEDNESDAY

TO DO

○ THURSDAY

○ FRIDAY

○ SATURDAY / SUNDAY

○ MONDAY

SUSTAINABLE ACTIONS

○ TUESDAY

○ WEDNESDAY

TO DO

○ THURSDAY

○ FRIDAY

○ SATURDAY / SUNDAY

○ MONDAY

SUSTAINABLE ACTIONS

_____

_____

○ TUESDAY

_____

_____

_____

_____

○ WEDNESDAY

_____

TO DO

_____

○ THURSDAY

_____

_____

_____

_____

○ FRIDAY

_____

_____

_____

_____

○ SATURDAY / SUNDAY

_____

_____

_____

○ MONDAY

SUSTAINABLE ACTIONS

○ TUESDAY

○ WEDNESDAY

TO DO

○ THURSDAY

○ FRIDAY

○ SATURDAY / SUNDAY

○ MONDAY

SUSTAINABLE ACTIONS
_____
_____
_____
_____
_____
_____

○ TUESDAY

○ WEDNESDAY

TO DO
_____
_____
_____
_____
_____
_____

○ THURSDAY

_____
_____

○ FRIDAY

_____
_____
_____

○ SATURDAY / SUNDAY

_____
_____
_____

○ MONDAY

SUSTAINABLE ACTIONS

○ TUESDAY

○ WEDNESDAY

TO DO

○ THURSDAY

○ FRIDAY

○ SATURDAY / SUNDAY

○ MONDAY

SUSTAINABLE ACTIONS

○ TUESDAY

○ WEDNESDAY

TO DO

○ THURSDAY

○ FRIDAY

○ SATURDAY / SUNDAY

○ MONDAY

SUSTAINABLE ACTIONS

○ TUESDAY

○ WEDNESDAY

TO DO

○ THURSDAY

○ FRIDAY

○ SATURDAY / SUNDAY

○ MONDAY

SUSTAINABLE ACTIONS

○ TUESDAY

○ WEDNESDAY

TO DO

○ THURSDAY

○ FRIDAY

○ SATURDAY / SUNDAY

○ MONDAY

SUSTAINABLE ACTIONS

○ TUESDAY

○ WEDNESDAY

TO DO

○ THURSDAY

○ FRIDAY

○ SATURDAY / SUNDAY

○ MONDAY

SUSTAINABLE ACTIONS

○ TUESDAY

○ WEDNESDAY

TO DO

○ THURSDAY

○ FRIDAY

○ SATURDAY / SUNDAY

○ MONDAY

SUSTAINABLE ACTIONS

○ TUESDAY

○ WEDNESDAY

TO DO

○ THURSDAY

○ FRIDAY

○ SATURDAY / SUNDAY

○ MONDAY

SUSTAINABLE ACTIONS

○ TUESDAY

○ WEDNESDAY

TO DO

○ THURSDAY

○ FRIDAY

○ SATURDAY / SUNDAY

○ MONDAY

SUSTAINABLE ACTIONS

○ TUESDAY

○ WEDNESDAY

TO DO

○ THURSDAY

○ FRIDAY

○ SATURDAY / SUNDAY

○ MONDAY

○ TUESDAY

○ WEDNESDAY

○ THURSDAY

○ FRIDAY

○ SATURDAY / SUNDAY

SUSTAINABLE ACTIONS

TO DO

○ MONDAY

SUSTAINABLE ACTIONS

○ TUESDAY

○ WEDNESDAY

TO DO

○ THURSDAY

○ FRIDAY

○ SATURDAY / SUNDAY

○ MONDAY

SUSTAINABLE ACTIONS

○ TUESDAY

○ WEDNESDAY

TO DO

○ THURSDAY

○ FRIDAY

○ SATURDAY / SUNDAY

○ MONDAY

SUSTAINABLE ACTIONS

○ TUESDAY

○ WEDNESDAY

TO DO

○ THURSDAY

○ FRIDAY

○ SATURDAY / SUNDAY

○ MONDAY

SUSTAINABLE ACTIONS

○ TUESDAY

○ WEDNESDAY

TO DO

○ THURSDAY

○ FRIDAY

○ SATURDAY / SUNDAY

○ MONDAY

SUSTAINABLE ACTIONS

○ TUESDAY

○ WEDNESDAY

TO DO

○ THURSDAY

○ FRIDAY

○ SATURDAY / SUNDAY

○ MONDAY

SUSTAINABLE ACTIONS

○ TUESDAY

○ WEDNESDAY

TO DO

○ THURSDAY

○ FRIDAY

○ SATURDAY / SUNDAY

○ MONDAY

SUSTAINABLE ACTIONS

○ TUESDAY

○ WEDNESDAY

TO DO

○ THURSDAY

○ FRIDAY

○ SATURDAY / SUNDAY

○ MONDAY

SUSTAINABLE ACTIONS

○ TUESDAY

○ WEDNESDAY

TO DO

○ THURSDAY

○ FRIDAY

○ SATURDAY / SUNDAY

Made in the USA
Las Vegas, NV
12 September 2024

95168334R00057